Exploring Acadia National Park

Solve Problems Involving the Four Operations

Jonathan Juszkiewicz

NEW YORK

Published in 2015 by The Rosen Publishing Group, Inc.
29 East 21st Street, New York, NY 10010

Book Design: Mickey Harmon

Photo Credits: Cover, p. 9 Zack Frank/Shutterstock.com; pp. 3–24 (background) S-F/Shutterstock.com; p. 5 spirit of
america/Shutterstock.com; p. 7 Boston Globe/Contributor/Boston Globe/Getty Images; p. 11 Doug Lemke/
Shutterstock.com; p. 13 Romiana Lee/Shutterstock.com; p. 15 Gavriel Jecan/The Image Bank/Getty Images; p. 17 Carol
Heesen/Shutterstock.com; p. 19 jo Crebbin/Shutterstock.com; p. 21 Pecold/Shutterstock.com; p. 22 Jearu/
Shutterstock.com.

Library of Congress Cataloging-in-Publication Data

Juszkiewicz, Jonathan, author.
Exploring Acadia National Park: solve problems involving the four operations / Jonathan Juszkiewicz.
    pages cm. — (Math masters. Operations and algebraic thinking)
Includes index.
ISBN 978-1-4777-4944-9 (pbk.)
ISBN 978-1-4777-4945-6 (6-pack)
ISBN 978-1-4777-6412-1 (library binding)
1. Word problems (Mathematics)—Juvenile literature. 2. Mathematics—Juvenile literature. 3. Acadia National Park
(Me.)—Juvenile literature. I. Title.
QA63.J87 2015
510—dc23
                          2014003116

Manufactured in the United States of America

CPSIA Compliance Information: Batch #WS15RC: For further information contact Rosen Publishing, New York, New York at 1-800-237-9932.

Contents

The Park's History

Acadia National Park has a rich history and a wide **variety** of plants and animals. It's located on Maine's Atlantic coast. The park includes much of Mount Desert Island, and one of its most famous features is Cadillac Mountain. This mountain reaches a height of 1,530 feet (466 m).

In 1919, this land became the first national park east of the Mississippi River. It was called Lafayette National Park at that time.

In 1929, Lafayette National Park was renamed Acadia National Park. "Acadia" was the name given to this land when the French discovered it in the 1600s.

In the 1880s, wealthy people began building estates, or large country homes, on Mount Desert Island. For more than 40 years, some of the most powerful families in America had estates there.

Let's say there were 2 estates on the island. Then, 3 new estates were built on the island each year for the next 5 years. How many estates would there be altogether after the 5 years were over? You can find the answer by breaking the question into 2 steps.

You can use **parentheses** to show what part of a math problem, or equation, you're going to do first. In this equation, you need to multiply 5 by 3 first. Then, add the 2 estates that were originally on the island. This gives you an answer of 17 total estates.

$$(5 \times 3) + 2 = ?$$

step 1: $5 \times 3 = 15$

step 2: $15 + 2 = 17$

Order of Operations

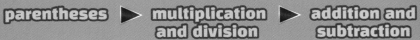

parentheses ▶ multiplication and division ▶ addition and subtraction

7

Many of the estates on Mount Desert Island were destroyed in a huge fire that swept across the island in 1947. The fire lasted from October 17 until November 14.

Large parts of the forests of Acadia National Park were also destroyed. However, new trees soon began to grow. An area of the park with 50 trees might have had that number cut in half. Then, 100 new trees grew there. How many total trees would be in that area of the park?

You can use a letter, such as *x*, to stand for the missing number in an equation. To **solve** this equation, first you must find out what half of 50 is. Divide 50 by 2, which equals 25. Then, add that number to the 100 new trees. The answer is 125 trees.

$$(50 \div 2) + 100 = x$$

step 1: $50 \div 2 = 25$

step 2: $25 + 100 = 125$

A Variety of Trees

Since the fire of 1947, there's a greater variety of trees in Acadia National Park. There are still many spruce and fir trees, just as there were before the fire. However, many other kinds of trees began to grow in the park, including maple and oak.

On a hike in Acadia National Park, you might count 95 trees altogether. That number includes 6 groups of trees with 12 oak trees in each group. The rest are maple trees. How many maple trees did you count?

In order to find the number of maple trees, you have to subtract the number of oak trees from the total number of trees. The number of oak trees is 72 because that's what you get when you multiply 6 by 12. Then, you subtract 72 from 95 to get 23 maple trees.

$$(6 \times 12) + x = 95$$

step 1: $6 \times 12 = 72$

step 2: $72 + x = 95$

$x = 95 - 72$

$x = 23$

Along the Ocean

Acadia National Park has over 40 miles (64 km) of rocky shoreline along the Atlantic Ocean. Imagine walking 4 miles a day for a week. After the week was over, how much farther would you need to walk to reach 40 miles?

To solve this equation, you first need to know there are 7 days in 1 week. Then, multiply 4 miles per day by 7 days. That gives you 28 miles walked in 1 week. Finally, subtract the miles you walked from the total miles to get 12 miles.

In the original equation, you can use m to stand for the missing number of miles.

$$(4 \times 7) + m = 40$$

step 1: $4 \times 7 = 28$

step 2: $28 + m = 40$

$m = 40 - 28$

$m = 12$

Some beaches in Acadia National Park are cobble beaches. These are formed when strong waves moved rocks from 1 part of the shoreline to another. The rocks are often made round and smooth by the force of the water.

On a part of the shoreline, 195 small rocks might be moved in 1 day, 212 moved on another day, and 75 moved on the third day. How many rocks are moved altogether? You can round the numbers to make a guess before solving the equation.

Rounding the numbers in an equation makes it easier to do math in your head. The answer you get will be an estimate, or an answer that's close to the actual answer. In this example, the number you get after rounding (475) is very close to the number you get when solving the real equation (482). Is 482 a reasonable answer based on your estimation? Yes!

$$195 + 212 + 75 = r$$

rounding	**solving**
$(200 + 200) + 75 = r$	$(195 + 212) + 75 = r$
step 1: 200 + 200 = 400	**step 1: 195 + 212 = 407**
step 2: 400 + 75 = 475	**step 2: 407 + 75 = 482**

Snapping Turtles

The Atlantic Ocean isn't the only body of water seen in Acadia National Park. There are many ponds in the park, too. Snapping turtles live in these ponds. Female snapping turtles can lay between 20 and 40 eggs at a time.

In Acadia National Park, 2 snapping turtles could lay eggs in nests near each other. In 1 nest, there are 38 eggs, and there are 24 in the other nest. If predators eat 11 eggs, how many total eggs are left?

Because the numbers in this equation are under 100, you can round them to the nearest 10 to get a quick estimate. The answers are very close. This tells us the answer is reasonable. ▶

rounding	solving
(40 + 20) - 10 = e	(38 + 24) - 11 = e
step 1: 40 + 20 = 60	step 1: 38 + 24 = 62
step 2: e = 60 − 10	step 2: e = 62 − 11
e = 50	e = 51

17

Birds in Acadia

Acadia National Park is also home to many species, or kinds, of birds. One kind of bird is the bald eagle. This bird is sometimes used as a **symbol** of the United States.

Let's say a bald eagle catches the same number of fish every day for 8 days. It catches 23 fish from a stream, and 17 from a lake. How many fish does the eagle collect in a single day? First, you have to find the total number of fish the eagle catches. Then, divide the number by 8 days.

The bald eagle catches 5 fish each day. Let's say you first rounded the 8 up to 10 to make the math problem easier to work with. What number do you get when you divide 40 by 10? Is it close to 5? If it is, your answer is reasonable.

$$(23 + 17) \div 8 = f$$

step 1: $23 + 17 = 40$

step 2: $f = 40 \div 8$
$f = 5$

Another bird that lives in Acadia National Park is the snowy owl. Snowy owls use their strong senses of sight and hearing to help them hunt. They hunt small **mammals**, fish, and even other birds. Unlike other owls, which hunt at night, snowy owls are active during the day.

At Acadia National Park, you could see 7 snowy owls a day for 2 days. If you saw 113 birds altogether during those 2 days, how many other birds did you see?

What steps would you take to solve this problem? How would you use rounding to **predict** or check your answer?

(2 x 7) + *b* = 113

So Many Animals!

Acadia National Park is a very popular place for people to visit if they want to see a variety of plants and animals. The park has mountains and beaches, as well as forests and wetlands. These different areas allow many different species of wildlife to make their home in the park. You can find fish, frogs, and turtles in the park's waters. You can see deer, chipmunks, and mice in its forests. You can even find harbor seals in the park!

Harbor seals can be found along the rocky shorelines of Acadia National Park.

Glossary

mammal (MAA-muhl) Any warm-blooded animal whose babies drink milk and whose body is covered with hair or fur.

parentheses (puh-REHN-thuh-seez) A pair of rounded marks used to group parts of a math problem.

predict (prih-DIHKT) To make a guess about an answer based on facts or knowledge.

solve (SAHLV) To find an answer for.

symbol (SIHM-buhl) Something that stands for something else.

variety (vuh-RY-uh-tee) A number or collection of different things.

Index

Due to the changing nature of Internet links, The Rosen Publishing Group, Inc., has developed an online list of websites related to the subject of this book. This site is updated regularly. Please use this link to access the list: www.powerkidslinks.com/mm/oat/acnp